ADAPTED TO SURVIVE

ANIMALS THAT HIDE

Angela Royston

Raintree
Chicago, Illinois

To contact Capstone Global Library please
phone 800-747-4992, or visit our website www.
capstonepub.com

Edited by Dan Nunn, Rebecca Rissman, and Helen
Cox Cannons
Designed by Jo Hinton-Malivoire
Original illustrations © Capstone Global Library Ltd
Picture research by Mica Brancic
Production by Helen McCreath
Originated by Capstone Global Library Ltd

**Library of Congress Cataloging-in-Publication
Data**
Royston, Angela, 1945- author.
  Animals that hide / Angela Royston.
    pages cm.—(Adapted to survive)
  Includes bibliographical references and index.
  ISBN 978-1-4109-6149-5 (hb)—ISBN 978-1-4109-
6156-3 (pb) 1. Camouflage (Biology)—Juvenile
literature. 2. Animals—Color—Juvenile literature. 3.
Animals—Adaptation—Juvenile literature. I. Title.

QL767.R69 2014
591.47'2—dc23   2013017639

Printed and bound in the USA.
3489

Acknowledgments
The author and publisher are grateful to the
following for permission to reproduce copyright
material: Alamy: FogStock, 10, Robert Canis, 27;
FLPA: Chris Mattison, 12, PR Gil/Minden, 13; Nature
Picture Library: Charlie Summers, 6, Doug Perrine,
19, 22, Edwin Giesbers, 23, John Cancalosi, 25, 29
bottom right, Ken Preston-Mafham/PREMAPHOTOS,
9, Kim Taylor, 7, Robert Thompson, 26, Steven
Kazlowski , 11, Tony Heald, 15, Wild Wonders of
Europe/Haarberg, 21; Shutterstock: Eric Isselee,
29 bottom left, Eugene Sim, 29 top right, Gary
C.Tognoni, 17, outdoorsman, 20, Sally Wallis, 14,
Sergey Uryadnikov, 18, TheRocky41, 16, 29 top left,
vicspacewalker, Cover; SuperStock: Bruce & Jan
Lichtenberger, 4, Minden Pictures, 5, 24, Steven
Kazlowski, 8

We would like to thank Michael Bright for his
invaluable help in the preparation of this book.

Every effort has been made to contact copyright
holders of any material reproduced in this book.
Any omissions will be rectified in subsequent
printings if notice is given to the publisher.

All the Internet addresses (URLs) given in this
book were valid at the time of going to press.
However, due to the dynamic nature of the
Internet, some addresses may have changed,
or sites may have changed or ceased to exist
since publication. While the author and publisher
regret any inconvenience this may cause readers,
no responsibility for any such changes can be
accepted by either the author or the publisher.

Some words are shown in bold, **like this**. You can find
out what they mean by looking in the glossary.

CONTENTS

GOOD AT HIDING

Many animals are good at hiding. Mice crawl through tiny gaps, crabs find shelter under stones on the seashore, and frightened rabbits run into their **burrows**. However, some animals hide by staying still and blending in with the background. This is called **camouflage**.

Hide and Seek
How and why
do animals use
camouflage to hide?

WHY DO ANIMALS HIDE?

Hiding helps an animal **survive**. **Camouflage** gives an extra advantage. It allows an animal to see other animals, without being seen by them. Both **predators** and **prey** use camouflage. A toad, for example, hides from birds and other predators, but it also hides from insects it eats!

leopard

ADAPTED TO HIDE

An **adaptation** is something special about an animal's body that helps it **survive**. **Camouflage** is an adaptation, because the animal's skin, fur, or feathers are the same coloring as the background or **habitat**.

ptarmigan

This blue shined grasshopper is so well camouflaged that it is almost impossible to see— until it moves!

POLAR BEARS

Polar bears and other Arctic animals have white fur to **camouflage** them against the ice and snow. Polar bears hunt for seals on the ice. They wait quietly until a seal comes above water to breathe. By the time the seal sees the bear, it is too late!

This polar bear is watching a hole in the ice. He is waiting for a seal to appear.

DESERT DISGUISE

Sidewinder snakes live in hot deserts. Their **scaly** skin is pink, orange, gray, or brown to match the sand where they live. Sidewinders hunt at night. During the day, they hide beneath the sand.

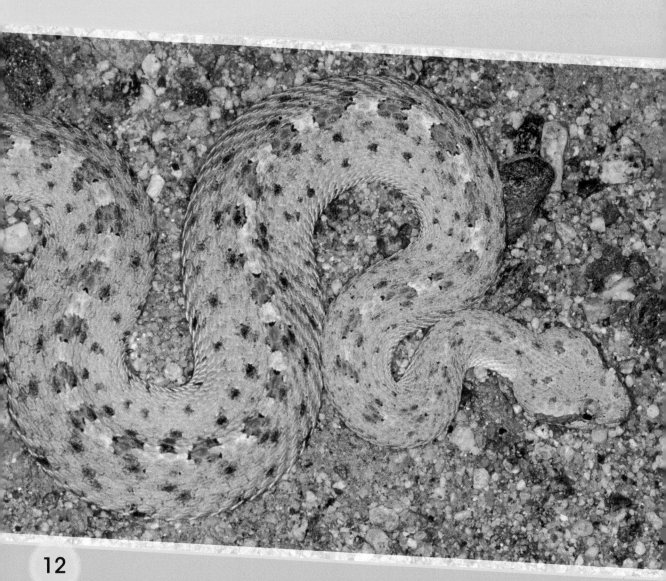

DID YOU KNOW?
Some sidewinders have short, scaly horns above each eye. These horns protect their eyes from sand when they are buried.

TIGER STRIPES

Tigers have orange and white fur with black stripes. They are easy to recognize, but the stripes **camouflage** them in the tropical forests where they live. A tiger hides in the **undergrowth** and waits for **prey**. Then it creeps up until it is near enough to pounce!

DID YOU KNOW?
No two tigers have the same pattern of stripes!

ZEBRA STRIPES

A zebra's black and white stripes do not blend in with the **grasslands** where they live! However, a zebra's stripes do protect it from **predators**. Zebras live together in herds. The stripes make it hard for the predator to pick out one zebra from the rest.

When a predator attacks, the herd runs away.

SHARKS

When a shark is seen from above, its dark back blends in with the dark sea below it.

Like many **predators**, sharks do not want to be spotted before they attack. Their dark backs and light bellies help hide them from **prey** above and below.

When a shark is seen from below, its light belly is **camouflaged** against the sky.

ARCTIC FOXES

Arctic foxes change color with the seasons. As summer comes and the snow melts, their white winter fur changes to brown or gray to blend in with the rocks. In fall, their white fur grows back.

It takes several weeks for an Arctic fox to change color.

QUICK CHANGE

Some animals can change color very quickly. Types of flatfish and cuttlefish hide from **predators** by changing their skin patterns to match the sand or stones below them. Some chameleons change color to **camouflage** themselves. They also change color when they are angry or scared, or to warm up or cool down.

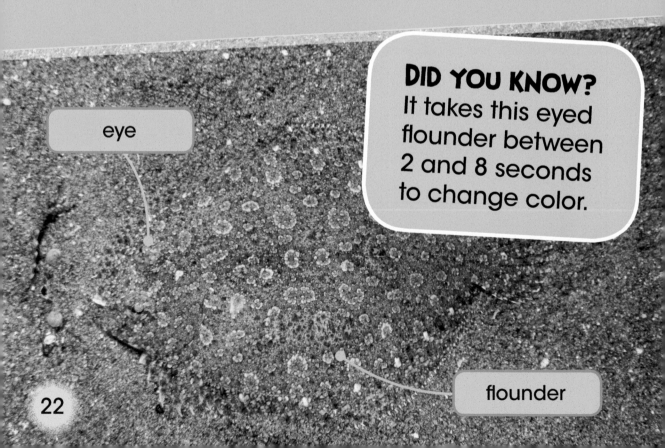

eye

flounder

chameleon

PLANTS OR INSECTS?

Some insects disguise themselves as parts of plants! Some look like leaves, and others look like twigs. They keep very still so that **predators** do not see them. Leaf insects are the same color as leaves, and they are shaped like leaves, too.

leaf insect

Ouch!
Thorn insects are
shaped just like thorns!

LOOKING FIERCE

Some insects use **camouflage** to stay safe by looking more dangerous. For example, when a bird attacks an elephant hawkmoth caterpillar, it is in for a surprise. The caterpillar pulls its head into its body to look like a snake with a large head and black eye patches!

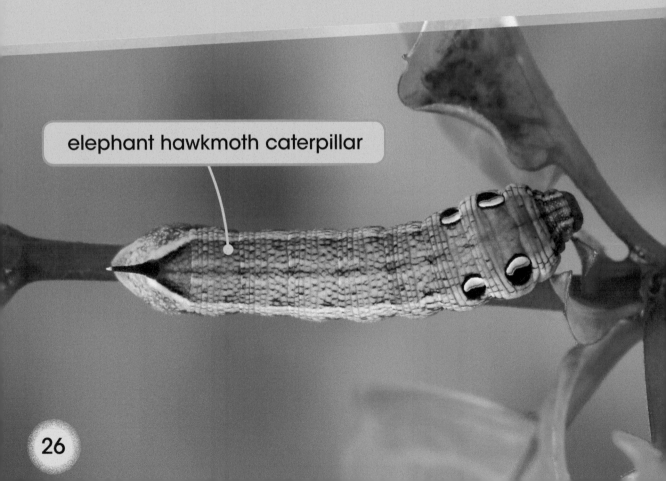

elephant hawkmoth caterpillar

eye patches

ANIMAL CHALLENGE

1. Which do you think is better **camouflaged**—a butterfly or a grasshopper?

2. What color are animals that live in rain forests most likely to be?

3. Why do you think that many animals that live in **grasslands** are brown, not green?

Invent your own camouflaged animal. First, decide what type of **habitat** it lives in, and then decide how you will help it hide. You can use the **adaptations** shown in the photos, or you can make up your own.

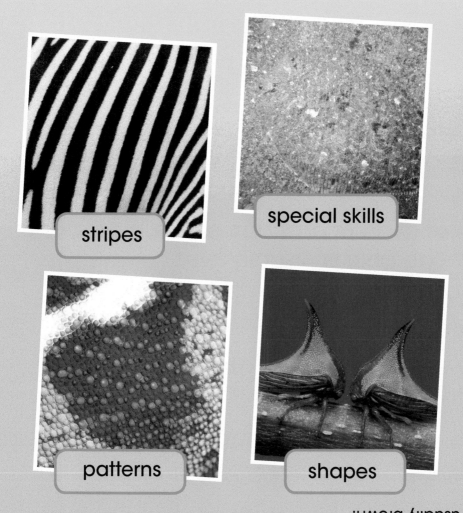

stripes

special skills

patterns

shapes

Answers to Animal Challenge

1. A grasshopper is well camouflaged against green plants, but most butterflies are not camouflaged.
2. Most rain forest animals are green or brown, like the leaves on the trees.
3. Dry grass is yellow or brown, so animals that live on dry grasslands are usually brown.

GLOSSARY

adaptation special thing about an animal's body that helps it survive in a particular way or in a particular habitat

burrow home dug below the surface of the ground by some types of animals

camouflage hide by blending in with the background or habitat

grassland area where the main plants are grass and there are few trees

habitat type of environment or landscape where an animal usually lives

predator animal that hunts and kills other animals for food

prey animal that is hunted and eaten by another animal

scaly covered with small, hard plates of skin

survive manage to go on living

undergrowth thick bushes and plants that grow beneath the trees in a forest

FIND OUT MORE

BOOKS

Riehecky, Janet. *Camouflage and Mimicry* (Animal Weapons and Defenses). Mankato, Minn.: Capstone, 2012.

Thomas, Isabel. *Remarkable Reptiles.* Chicago: Raintree, 2013.

Underwood, Deborah. *Creature Camouflage* (series). Chicago: Heinemann, 2011.

Wood, Alix. *Amazing Animal Camouflage.* New York: Windmill, 2013.

WEB SITES

FactHound offers a safe, fun way to find Internet sites related to this book. All of the sites on FactHound have been researched by our staff.

Here's all you do:
Visit www.facthound.com
Type in this code: 9781410961495

INDEX